GOAL
SQUAD

WIN THE CUP

GOAL SQUAD

WIN THE CUP

SCOTT ALLEN
ILLUSTRATED BY
LIDIA FERNANDEZ

■SCHOLASTIC

Published in the UK by Scholastic, 2026
Scholastic, Bosworth Avenue, Warwick, CV34 6UQ
Scholastic Ireland, 89E Lagan Road, Dublin Industrial
Estate, Glasnevin, Dublin, D11 HP5F

SCHOLASTIC and associated logos are trademarks and/or
registered trademarks of Scholastic Inc.

Text by Scott Allen © Scholastic, 2026
Cover and inside illustrations by Lidia Fernandez © Scholastic, 2026

ISBN 978 0702 34615 6

A CIP catalogue record for this book is available from the British Library.

All rights reserved.
This book is sold subject to the condition that it shall not, by way of trade or
otherwise, be lent, hired out or otherwise circulated in any form of binding
or cover other than that in which it is published. No part of this publication
may be reproduced, stored in a retrieval system, or transmitted in any form
or by any other means (electronic, mechanical, photocopying, recording or
otherwise), or used to train any artificial intelligence technologies without prior
written permission of Scholastic Limited. Subject to EU law, Scholastic Limited
expressly reserves this work from the text and data-mining exception.

Printed in the UK.
Paper made from wood grown in sustainable forests and other controlled sources.

10 9 8 7 6 5 4 3 2 1

This is a work of fiction. Any resemblance to actual people,
events or locales is entirely coincidental.

Scholastic does not have any control over and does not assume any
responsibility for any third-party websites or other platforms, or their content.

www.scholastic.co.uk

For safety or quality concerns:
UK: www.scholastic.co.uk/productinformation
EU: www.scholastic.ie/productinformation

*To Mum – your amazing cakes
are still better than football*

Chapter 1

The ball flicked the edge of the post and pinged into the top corner of the net...

GOAL SQUAD

The Eagles' players leaped about, punching the air with delight.

"WOOOOOOOOO-HOOOOOO!"

"C'mon, EAAAAAGGGLLLLEESSSSSS!"

"Ugggghhhhhhh," groaned Leo from the halfway line.

Their goalkeeper held his head in his hands. Josh had made lots of great diving saves in the match, but he couldn't stop that one.

Time was running out, and the Tigers were struggling near the bottom of the league table. Leo was their striker. He *had* to find a way to score. Shame he hadn't been playing very well all game.

He called towards the Tigers' left-winger. "We still have time to get a goal, Mo."

Mo gave him a thumbs up. "No problem! That goal was lucky."

Win the Cup!

Leo laughed, turned round – and bumped straight into the Eagles' big defender, Number Five, who had been marking him all game.

"No chance, bro," said Number Five gruffly. "There's no time left, and you'll soon be at the bottom of the table." Without waiting for a reply, he jogged off.

Leo waited until he was far enough away, then stuck his tongue out and blew a very quick, very secretive raspberry.

"Pfffffftttttttttt."

There! That made him feel much better.

GOAL SQUAD

The ref handed Leo the ball. It was time to kick the match off again.

"Three minutes left," she said as she raised the whistle to her lips and blew.

Leo tapped the ball to the Tigers' midfielder and captain, Frankie.

Frankie ran forward with the ball, then passed it to Mo, who was superfast and really good at dribbling. He beat two players and got ready to cross the ball. Leo could guess where it was headed and sprinted into the penalty area.

It was a perfect cross, and Leo stuck his boot out to volley the ball into the net... *That must be 1-1*, he thought.

"BOSHHHHHHH!!!" shouted Number Five as he threw himself at the ball, heading it over the crossbar and out for a corner.

Leo felt a lead weight drop into his stomach. An important chance missed.

"Still got time," said Mo as he collected the ball and took it towards the corner flag.

Frankie ran over to Leo and whispered, "That number five has been stopping you all match. If I put him off, you can deffo score."

Leo nodded.

GOAL SQUAD

"Hey, stop whispering," said Number Five.

"Just deciding who's going to score," replied Frankie. He started running round the penalty area in circles. "It'll probably be me."

The number five fell for Frankie's trick and began moving towards him, leaving Leo on his own. He might actually have a chance to score now!

But at the side of the pitch, the Tigers' coach, Tommy Socket, was talking to one of the substitutes, Olli, and pointing at the pitch. Olli thought he was the best striker in the team, even though it was Leo who always started every game. Leo felt a cold sweat creep up his back. If Tommy was talking to Olli, that meant he was thinking of bringing him on. Which meant Leo would have to come off. He didn't want that to happen before this important corner.

"Corner first, then substitutes," said the ref as though reading Leo's thoughts.

Phew! Leo breathed a sigh of relief. This was it, his last chance to get a goal and stay on the pitch.

Mo floated in a great corner. The ball hung in the air just long enough for Leo to get into the perfect position.

GOAL SQUAD

Bicycle or scissor kick? flashed through his mind. It was now or never. No more time to think.

Leo jumped up and launched himself towards the ball...

Chapter 2

Leo timed his scissor kick perfectly. His right foot met the ball with a satisfying thud, and it soared towards the top right-hand corner of the net.

GOAL SQUAD

That's definitely going in this time, Leo thought.

It was the last he saw of the ball before he face-planted on the grass.

The big number five had smashed right into Leo's legs and dumped him back on to the pitch. Immediately, a bolt of heat shot across his ankle.

Out of the corner of his eye, Leo saw the Eagles' goalkeeper reach … reach … REACH! With a final stretch, he flicked the ball over the crossbar. His fingers must have been made from elastic bands!

Leo groaned. It was still 1–0.

From across the pitch, he could make out the muffled sounds of the Eagles' team congratulating their keeper with slaps on the back.

"Oooohhh, what a save!" said a voice.

Win the Cup!

"You da man, Bobby!" cried another.

Leo tried to pull himself up off the grass, but he was all stiff. Something wasn't right. A red-hot throbbing feeling started pulsing from Leo's sock. He looked down and could see a massive lump just above the top of his boot from where he'd been tackled.

Leo groaned again.

GOAL SQUAD

PEEEEEEEEEEEPPPPPPPPP! went the ref's whistle.

"Foul. Penalty to the Tigers," said the ref, pointing to the spot.

Leo's stomach did a little excited somersault. For a few seconds, he forgot about the pain in his ankle. Now he could finally get the equalizer. He always took the penalties and hadn't missed one all season.

"No way, ref!" shouted the Eagles' number five. "That was never a penalty."

"Penalty," said the ref again. "Hurry up, it's nearly full time."

The number five stomped away, muttering under his breath, "You are blind, ref."

"And you are about to be booked, Number Five," shouted the ref, reaching

Win the Cup!

into her pocket and holding up a yellow card. "It was a penalty and I am *not* blind."

"I never said anything," Number Five cried as his teammates pulled him away. "It wasn't me, it was that guy!" He pointed at Leo, still on the ground and rubbing his throbbing ankle. It felt like someone was whacking it with a big metal spoon.

Mo and Frankie came over and helped Leo back to his feet.

"You OK?" asked Mo.

"Yeah, think I'll be all right," said Leo. "Got to take this penalty, haven't I?"

"You'll smash it, no problem," said Frankie. "Yeah, the Eagles' keeper is good, but nobody can stop one of your penalties."

Leo felt bubbles of happiness travel up his spine. Frankie believed in him! He began to walk over to the ball that was now sitting on the penalty spot.

But as soon as his studs sank into the grass, the feeling of another twenty metal spoons began whacking his ankle – this time faster and harder.

"YEEEOOOOOWWWW," yelped Leo, lifting his foot quickly off the ground.

"Aw, man! Your ankle has gone massive," said Mo, bending down to inspect it. "You can't take a penalty with that."

"Hurry up," said the ref, looking at Leo, Mo and Frankie.

Tommy Socket began shouting from the sidelines and circling his hands over one another – the signal for a sub. Leo

Win the Cup!

could feel his knees going wobbly. He was coming off. Worse still, Olli was coming on.

"Leo, off you come, please," Tommy Socket called across the pitch. Immediately, Olli appeared on the sidelines and began hopping up and down and doing leg-stretching exercises like an overexcited kangaroo. His kit and boots were the neatest ever, with not a speck of mud. There were rumours that a special cleaning team came to his house and washed his kit after every match. Others said his dad bought him brand-new kit and boots for each game.

GOAL SQUAD

Leo hopped off the pitch to the side of the goal, an arm slung around Mo's shoulder. Tommy Socket ran over with his big red bucket and sponge, and started soaking Leo's sock with water. It wasn't helping.

"I'll go and get some ice," he said, and sprinted away.

Frankie readied himself to take the penalty. But Olli ran up and barged him out of the way. His voice floated over from the goalposts.

"I'm taking this," Leo heard him announce. "Socket said."

"Did he?" Frankie said. "It's usually me after Leo."

Had their coach really said that? He didn't usually make last-minute changes.

"No, me," said Olli, cutting Frankie off. "I've got more goals than you this season

Win the Cup!

and I've scored against this goalkeeper before."

It was too late now for Frankie to argue. The ref was waving him out of the penalty area in front of the goal. Olli was going to take it.

Olli brushed some mud off the ball, took four steps back and swept his hair across his head four times. His hair, like his kit and boots, had to be just right. Then he took a deep breath and waited.

PEEEEEEEPPPPPP! went the ref's whistle, her face turning red as she blew.

Olli charged up to the ball, stopped dead still – then quickly flicked it into a corner of the net. Leo had to admit, it was the perfect pen. The keeper had no chance.

1–1.

"Yessssssssssssssssssss!" shouted Olli into

GOAL SQUAD

the sky with his arms out wide.

The ref blew the final whistle.

The Tigers' players flooded the pitch, lifting Olli on to their shoulders. Leo tried to follow, but it would have taken him a week to hop there with his bad ankle.

Win the Cup!

He tugged down his sock. His ankle had gone bright purple, the most purple thing Leo had ever seen in his whole life.

"Oh no," he whispered. "Is my football career over already?"

Chapter 3

After the match, Tommy Socket sat everyone down in the changing room to talk about the final few weeks of the season.

Win the Cup!

The Tigers were in big trouble near the bottom of the table. Losing any matches could see them relegated from the top division.

Tommy pulled a piece of paper out of his pocket and pinned it to the noticeboard. It was covered in squiggles and numbers, and looked like he had written it upside down on a roller coaster. There was a league table, with all twelve teams in a long list with their points next to them. The top eight teams were written in blue pen, teams nine and ten in green, and the bottom two in red.

Leo had a bag of ice cubes on his ankle, but he managed to lean forward enough to see that the Tigers were in red, second from bottom and in the relegation zone. His stomach turned over. He'd thought the 1–1 draw against the Eagles would have been enough to keep them above the drop.

Win the Cup!

"Good result out there, Tigers. We really needed to get that point," said Tommy Socket. He jabbed his finger at the piece of paper. "But as you can see, we are now in the relegation zone, as the Volcanoes and the Cobras both won today."

The team muttered to each other. Leo readjusted his ice pack. It wasn't working very well. The throbbing in his ankle was getting worse, and the bright purple colour now had nasty yellowy-green patches.

"We have three games left to get out of the relegation zone," continued Tommy. "And we need the teams around us not to win."

Frankie raised his hand. "Aren't we playing the Volcanoes and the Cobras in the next two games?"

"That's right," said Tommy. "Good knowledge, Frankie."

GOAL SQUAD

"If I play all the games, we'll deffo win," said Olli. "Especially as Leo got himself injured."

"Shhhh, Olli," Frankie hissed. "It wasn't his fault."

Leo gave his friend a smile to say, *Thank you.*

"I'm just saying," Olli continued. "I'll *have* to play all the games if Leo's ankle is broken."

Why did Olli have the ability to make everything sound like Leo's fault?

"Leo was brave to win that penalty," said Tommy. "Sometimes you have to put the team first, and Leo did that."

Win the Cup!

Leo felt a warmth of pride rise up through his body. He always wanted to play well for everyone, not just score goals.

"And if we want to win the next three games, we all have to put the team first." He gave Olli a long look. "That includes you."

Olli's cheeks went red and he lowered his head.

"But remember, everyone!" said Tommy. "The last three games aren't all about fighting relegation. If we play well enough, we could sneak into eighth position. That's the last end-of-season cup qualification place."

The changing room burst into excited chatter. Leo fist-bumped Mo. They had both dreamed about lifting the end-of-season cup since they joined the club, aged six.

"OK, guys, I'll see you back here on Wednesday night for the next game. Make sure you get plenty of rest. Eat lots of vegetables and drink lots of water. Remember, cauliflower can be your friend ... even if it smells like farts."

The Tigers' players laughed and began packing up their kit. It was time to go home and prepare!

Win the Cup!

Mo, Frankie and a few other players went over to Leo before they left to check if he was OK.

"I'm fine," he said. "Don't worry about me." But he knew he wasn't.

"Your mum on her way?" Tommy asked.

Leo nodded. "She'll be here any moment."

Soon, the room was totally empty apart from Leo, his ice pack and one muddy sock that had been left on the floor.

Leo took another quick peek at his ankle. *Yuck*, he thought.

The door burst open and Leo's mum appeared, dressed in a luminous jacket, green trousers and boots. Slung over her shoulder was a large red bag with a big green cross in the middle. Luckily for Leo, his mum was a paramedic.

"Hi, Mum," he said, his voice low and grumpy.

"Aw, poor you," she said, giving him a cuddle. "Let's see what we've got here, then."

She removed the ice pack and studied Leo's ankle, asking lots of questions about how he felt.

Then she put the ice pack back and came to sit beside him on the bench. She took a deep breath.

"I've good news and bad news," she said. "Which do you want first?"

Thoughts raced through Leo's head. Would his foot have to be sawn off? Or even his whole leg? He'd heard injured players had

Win the Cup!

to eat lots of green vegetables. Would he have to eat broccoli for the rest of his life? He hated broccoli – even more than he hated cauliflower.

"Leo," said Mum, snapping him back into the changing room. "Which do you want first?"

"The good news," said Leo.

Leo's mum smiled. "The good news is that it's not broken or fractured."

"I won't need it sawed off, then?"

Leo's mum laughed. "No, not today. I don't even have a saw in my bag."

"Phew," said Leo, and he stopped feeling sweaty around his neck.

"However," continued Mum, "it's a bad bruise, and you'll have to rest it for at least a week."

"A week!" Leo cried.

"Yes, a week, maybe more."

GOAL SQUAD

"Maybe more!" Leo cried again, bashing the back of his head against the wall in frustration. "But it's a really important match on Wednesday. I have to play. We need to win."

"You'll make the injury much worse if you try and play. I'll tell your coach that you have to miss the game."

Leo dropped his head in his hands. This was a nightmare. He was the Tigers' top striker.

Win the Cup!

The team needed him to help them get out of the relegation zone and qualify for the end-of-season cup. What were his friends going to think? He'd let them all down.

Chapter 4

Four days later, Leo was sitting on the sidelines with his foot resting on a little table. He was dressed in his black team tracksuit, with a big roaring Tiger badge on his chest. His boots were in a bag beside him.

Win the Cup!

The bruise on his ankle was much better. Mum was right – it needed lots of rest, ice and to be up in the air for some reason. He also needed to eat ice cream. Lots of ice cream. He'd found that mint choc chip was the best medicine – better than vanilla, anyway.

Leo wasn't allowed to play the match against the Volcanoes, but he had told Tommy Socket he was ready if there was an emergency need for a top goalscoring striker.

Now the Tigers were deep in the second half, and the score was 1-1.

Mo had scored a brilliant goal, dribbling round three players before lobbing the goalkeeper from just outside the penalty area. But the Volcanoes had quickly hit back, scoring from a corner.

GOAL SQUAD

"Think you could use me in the last fifteen minutes?" Leo asked Tommy Socket as he walked up and down the sidelines.

Tommy laughed. "Nice try, Leo," he said. "You know I can't do that, especially as your mum will pull my ears off if I do."

"You scared of my mum?" Leo said, and smiled for the first time since the match against the Eagles.

Their coach pretended to bite his fingernails and look worried. "Always." Then he began clapping and shouting encouragement at the Tigers' players on the pitch. There wasn't long to go, and they had to win the game.

Win the Cup!

The Tigers were bombarding the Volcanoes' goal. Leo felt his legs tingle with eagerness. Oh, to have been out there! Mo had fired in five shots. Frankie had nearly scored a goal but hit the post. Olli had hardly touched the ball all game but was still telling everyone what to do as though he was the captain. Leo hoped that the team's real captain, Frankie, couldn't hear.

Then Olli's moment finally came. One of the Volcanoes' defenders tried to get the ball back to the keeper but didn't put enough power on the pass.

Olli nipped across the pitch and intercepted the ball. He was now one-on-one with the keeper.

The keeper was one of the biggest in the league, but he was too slow and couldn't get close to Olli. The striker dribbled round him and whacked the ball into the empty net.

2-1!

The Tigers' players went wild and Olli sprinted off the pitch with his arms high in the air. He threw himself into a knee slide, and the rest of the team jumped on top of him. Leo wished he could have joined in, hurling into the pile of limbs.

Win the Cup!

The ref had to blast the whistle several times to get the game started again.

The Tigers' players peeled themselves off the pitch and trotted back to their positions.

Olli picked himself up off the ground. He ran down the side of the pitch and stopped right in front of Leo.

Leo was about to say, "Well done on the goal," when Olli leaped into the air and shouted, "Siuuuu!" just as he landed.

He turned to Leo. "You could never have scored that," he said with a laugh. "Especially not with your massive INJURY."

Leo felt a burning fire of rage fill his head. He clenched his fists and tried to get off the bench, but it began to wobble and tipped over, throwing Leo on to the grass.

GOAL SQUAD

"Ha, look at that," said Olli. "You can't even get off the bench. How are you going to play in the next match? There's no chance, especially as I'm the top goalscorer in this team now."

Leo looked to see if Tommy Socket had heard, but he was busy giving instructions to one of the Tigers' players. Olli ran off to join the others, leaving Leo to climb back to his feet. He watched as Olli took the ball and placed it down on the turf, ready to start again.

That was the second time Olli had said something mean to a teammate. Leo folded his arms and shook his head. Olli might be able to score goals, but he didn't know how to be nice. The only problem was ... Leo had no way of proving it.

Win the Cup!

Leo looked at his ankle. *C'mon, ankle*, he thought. *You've got to get better. I need to help the team. Olli is only out for himself.*

Chapter 5

Frankie was waiting outside the changing room when Leo arrived for the match against the Cobras.

"Have you heard?" Frankie said in a rush.

"Heard what?" replied Leo.

Frankie looked over his shoulder, as though he was about to tell the biggest secret of his life or admit that he puts ketchup on his cereal.

Win the Cup!

"There's a scout coming to watch the game today," he whispered.

"A scout?" Leo echoed, yelping in surprise.

"Shhhhhh!" Frankie hissed. "My mum's boyfriend's brother's plumber told me, but we can't have everyone knowing – it's a secret. A massive secret. I'm not telling anyone."

"You just told me."

"Ah yes," said Frankie, rubbing his chin. "I might have told Mo too."

Mo bounded round the corner swinging his boots in a grotty supermarket bag. He called it his "lucky bag".

"Have you heard about the scout?" he said to Leo.

"Shhhh!" whispered Frankie. "It's supposed to be a secret."

"Is it?" said Mo. "I might have told Josh, by mistake."

GOAL SQUAD

"Doh!" said Frankie, slapping his forehead.

"And maybe Noah," continued Mo. "Possibly Azim."

"You told me too," said Olli, popping his head out of the dressing-room window. "He's deffo here to see me."

Leo glanced over at the supporters who had turned up to watch the match. It was mainly the families or carers of Tigers players. He could see Josh's younger brother picking his nose and secretly rubbing it on the backs of people's coats as usual.

There was a cluster of other people he didn't know. They were probably the Cobras' mums and dads. The scout could be with them.

Then he spotted a man sitting on his own by the corner flag. He was wearing a flat cap, sunglasses and a big black coat. He

Win the Cup!

was rummaging around in his inside pocket, looking for something. Maybe his notepad or phone to get all the info on the Tigers.

Leo looked down at his ankle, and balanced on one leg to twist it around in the air, testing for any pain. It was still sore, but felt much better than before. But because of Olli's goal against the Volcanoes, Tommy Socket had announced that Olli would start the match. Leo was going to be the sub. He didn't know much about football scouts, but one thing he did know ... they probably didn't take much notice of subs.

⚽

Leo spent the first half of the game jogging up and down the side of the pitch to make himself look as fit as possible.

It was still 0–0 at half-time, but the Tigers were the much better side. They'd had loads of shots on target. Unfortunately, the Cobras' goalkeeper was also playing brilliantly.

The second half started, and Leo was still waiting on the sidelines. Then a long kick down the pitch from the Tigers' goalkeeper, Josh, was missed by a Cobras defender. Mo collected the ball and dribbled into the

Win the Cup!

area. He sidestepped the goalkeeper and squared it to Olli, who smashed it in the top right-hand corner of the net.

Tigers 1   Cobras 0

The team went wild and Leo punched the air! The Tigers were on fire! Then his hand dropped to his side as he realized... *If Olli keeps scoring, I might not get a game today.* Tommy never substituted goalscorers.

He slumped down on one of the benches by the side of the pitch, zipped his tracksuit all the way up to his chin, and folded his arms.

GOAL SQUAD

Tommy turned and looked at him.

"What are you doing?" he said.

"Sitting down," said Leo.

"Why?"

"Cos we scored and you won't need me now."

"Did I say that?"

"No ... but I can tell."

Tommy laughed. "Don't be a lemon. This is exactly why I need you." He turned back to inspect the game. "There's still lots of time left, and we've already started defending too deep to stop them scoring. The Cobras are now taking lots of long-range shots."

A Cobras midfielder had a shot from the edge of the penalty area that Josh had to dive at full stretch to save.

"Great save, Josh!" shouted Tommy, clapping his hands together. He turned back

Win the Cup!

to Leo. "We need another couple of goals to win this game and to put some pressure at the Cobras' end of the pitch. I've spoken with your mum and she says you're ready. Get that tracksuit off and stop looking so grumpy."

Leo's heart did a flip, and he jumped up. His tracksuit was off in a flash, and his sore ankle nearly forgotten.

⚽

Leo was back! And this time, he was playing as striker alongside Olli. A very tired-looking Olli. But Leo felt fresh, like a new pair of trainers.

"C'mon!" Leo called over to him. "We need another goal."

But Olli looked the other way.

The ball landed at Leo's feet. Quickly, he passed it on to Mo, using the foot where he'd picked up the injury. Immediately, a shot of pain sparked through Leo's body, but it didn't hurt that much and quickly went away. Leo felt as though he could take on the world!

He raced into the penalty area. Mo passed the ball back and he fired off a snapshot towards the Cobras' goal. Unfortunately, it was an easy save for their keeper.

Win the Cup!

"Good stuff, Leo! Keep the pressure up!" Tommy called over.

Over the next ten minutes, Leo had another three shots saved by the Cobras' keeper, but he was getting closer and closer to getting one in. *I'm so nearly there!* he thought.

As they waited for a goal-kick to be taken, Frankie jogged over and slapped Leo on the back.

"You've got this, Leo," he said. "I can feel it. We need at least one more goal. I reckon the keeper is a bit weaker down to his left."

Leo nodded. Frankie was excellent at spotting things in the game that he hadn't noticed. That's why he was the captain.

Five minutes to go, and the Tigers were bombarding the Cobras' goal. Mo was having an amazing game. The Cobras couldn't get near him!

GOAL SQUAD

He was firing over cross after cross, shot after shot, but the Cobras' keeper was too good.

Frankie pinged in a bobbling shot from the edge of the penalty area. It skipped and bounced awkwardly towards the bottom left corner and this time the keeper struggled to get down to stop it.

The ball bounced out of his hands and away from his body. Leo was the fastest to the fumble and darted over to the ball, flicking it over the keeper and into the net!

Tigers 2   Cobras 0

The Tigers' players leaped all around Leo as he tried to celebrate. He felt as though he was walking on a cloud … a very muddy cloud of grass.

Chapter 6

After the match, the Tigers' players sat on the grass, drinking cartons of apple juice. Leo could see the man from earlier talking to the Cobras' goalkeeper.

Win the Cup!

The two of them shook hands and the stranger began walking towards the Tigers.

Leo felt a sharp dig in the side of his body. It was Frankie's elbow.

"I reckon that's the scout," he said.

"That's definitely the scout," Olli said, leaning in. "And he's here for me. I scored and had loads of shots." He was doing it again! Olli did like to talk a lot – about himself.

"So did Leo," Frankie pointed out.

"My goal was better. His was just a tap-in after the keeper dropped it. This might be one of my last games for the Tigers before I go into the big time."

The man arrived by their side. "Hi, everyone, I'm Brian."

The Tigers' players muttered hello back.

"I'm from a football club just along the river," Brian said. "You might have heard

GOAL SQUAD

about us... Westwood Flyers."

The Tigers' players all gasped – that was one of the biggest teams in the professional league.

Brian's glance travelled from face to face, eyes bright. "And I need to talk to one of you."

Olli started to push himself off the grass. He was so sure he was going to be picked.

Leo could feel butterflies dancing in his stomach. What if he was picked too? He had scored and taken lots of shots, but was it enough? Olli's words from earlier wormed into his brain. Olli was right – he'd only managed one goal. He looked down at his ankle. If he hadn't been injured, he would have been able to play the whole game and might have scored a few more goals.

He glanced at Frankie and Mo. Maybe the

Win the Cup!

scout wanted one of them. They were both really good players.

Frankie was a brilliant captain, great at tackling and passing, and was always in the thick of the action. Mo was fast, an amazing dribbler and crosser of the ball. He also had loads of tricks that were almost impossible to stop.

Or maybe Josh, the goalkeeper. He had made some great saves in the second half, but hadn't been that busy in the first.

Then there was Olli. Surely not him. Leo was a much better striker, but Olli was always telling anyone who'd listen how great he was. Leo preferred to let his feet do the talking. But his feet hadn't had much chance to talk today.

Brian cleared his throat. "So, I'm here to talk to...'

GOAL SQUAD

He took a long pause, and everyone held their breath. His glance ranged from one player to the next, taking them in one by one. This was agony! Even Tommy Socket looked nervous, rubbing his chin over and over.

"... Mo," he said, finally.

Mo's mouth dropped open. "I can't believe it!" he cried, slapping his hands together.

Leo felt a broad smile break out over his face.

Win the Cup!

Tommy started clapping. "Well done, Mo."

The team started slapping Mo on the back. His cheeks flushed bright red.

The only person who wasn't clapping was Olli. His face was scrunched up. There could have been steam coming out of his ears he looked so angry.

Leo felt really happy for Mo. He was easily one of the Tigers' best players this season

and had assisted with lots of goals. He'd had a brilliant game against the Cobras too.

Then Leo had a brand-new thought. Depending on what the scout said, his friend may or may not be leaving the Tigers! He might even be joining Westwood Flyers. Leo might never play with him again.

"Luckily for us, Mo won't be having his trial with Westwood Flyers straight away," Tommy announced. "They will let him play with us for the last league games, and if we make it to the end-of-season cup."

Leo sighed. That was good news. Without Mo, they were certain to be relegated.

"Sadly, I do have a bit of bad news," Tommy continued. "Even though we beat the Cobras, it's really tight at the bottom of the league."

He held up his tablet so that everyone could see.

GOAL SQUAD

"If we beat the Sharks in the last league game of the season, we stay up and could qualify for the end-of-season cup."

The team chattered among themselves.

"But if we lose, we won't qualify for the cup," their coach said. "The only problem is, the Sharks are top of the table. They're the best team in the division."

Chapter 7

It was cold, wet and windy on the final day of the season. The rain felt like ice when Leo arrived at the ground.

This was the kind of day where any normal person would be watching TV with a massive bag of sweets, not looking out of a changing-room window at puddles filling with mud.

GOAL SQUAD

Leo could see Olli sitting in his dad's massive car, waiting for the rain to stop. He had a new haircut, and it looked good. Leo's mum cut his hair over the kitchen sink.

He looked back into the changing room to see Tommy Socket pin the team sheet on the noticeboard. Tigers players crowded round, pointing out names. Mo was clutching his lucky supermarket bag, though he didn't need it now – not after his chat with the scout.

Leo didn't have to go over to know that he'd be on the bench again. Tommy always played with one striker, and he'd start with Olli as he'd scored first last week.

Frankie trotted up to Leo. He had a big smile on his face.

"What are you standing back here for, grumpy pants?"

Win the Cup!

"No reason," replied Leo.

"Is it because you think you aren't in the starting line-up?"

"Dunno," said Leo with a shrug.

"Well, turn those grumpy pants inside out and throw them out of the window," Frankie said, laughing. "You're on the team."

"You what?" Leo raced over to the team sheet. His ankle didn't even hurt any more!

GOAL SQUAD

It was true. There was Leo's name in thick black pen in the striker's position at the top of the team sheet.

Leo was so happy he thought his head might pop off. This was his chance to save the Tigers from relegation and qualify for the cup.

Then he saw another name next to his … Olli.

For the first time this season, the Tigers were playing with two strikers.

"We need to win today's game, and that means we need lots of goals," said Tommy, appearing next to Leo. "I need both my strikers on tip-top form today. No funny business."

"Yes, Tommy," Leo said. He could feel his feet tingling with excitement. They wanted to get out there and score some goals.

Win the Cup!

Olli walked into the dressing room and looked at the team sheet. He scrunched up his face.

"Your foot better not be broken any more," he said to Leo.

Leo lifted his foot and waggled it in front of Olli.

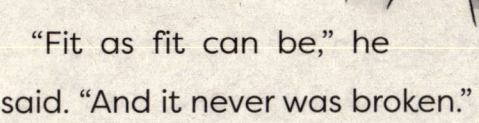

"Fit as fit can be," he said. "And it never was broken."

"Ugh, but it stinks like a baby's nappy with three massive poos in it," said Olli, holding his nose as he walked off.

Leo watched him go over to his bench. There was nothing – absolutely nothing! – that Olli could say or do today to ruin things. Leo was back in the game!

GOAL SQUAD

The league table didn't lie. The Sharks were a great team. They spent nearly the whole first half attacking the Tigers' goal. Now, it was half-time and it was still 0-0.

Josh stopped shot after shot, making fingertip saves, blocking with his legs and big punches. Leo thought he must have turned into an octopus overnight – his arms and legs were everywhere.

Frankie had an amazing game too. He was busy making crunching tackles, making important blocks, and he cleared the ball off the line not once but twice!

But at the other end of the pitch Leo and Olli had hardly touched the ball.

Olli had booted one shot over the bar when it would have been easier to pass it to Mo to score, and Leo had put a volley wide when he

Win the Cup!

should have hit the target.

That had been the total number of chances for the Tigers. As they walked back on to the pitch, Leo dug the toe of his boot into the turf in frustration. 0-0. It was not good enough. They needed goals and quick.

Leo could feel the pressure weighing down on his shoulders.

Tommy held back the team to whisper one last piece of advice. "Go long!" he said. "Kick the ball up the pitch quick."

With the sound of the ref's whistle, the game exploded into action again. Noah passed the ball to Frankie who quickly launched it as far as he could towards Leo.

GOAL SQUAD

Leo chested it down and turned. It was the best bit of skill he'd done all match. He moved the ball from his left foot to his right, dribbled forward a few metres, took aim and – *whoosh!* – curled a great shot towards the goal.

That's going in! The keeper can't reach it! he thought as it flew through the air. *It just needs to get over those Sharks players.*

The ball wobbled a bit in the wind but was still headed towards the top corner of the goal. Sharks players leaped up to get near the ball. It was a mad scramble, but they couldn't get near. It was going in!

Then, another figure appeared – in a black-and-orange kit.

No!

Win the Cup!

It was Olli. He was trying to knock the ball in! But he didn't need to, it was fine if he just...

Boing!

The ball sprang off Olli's head, then off the goalpost – and on to the grass beyond the crossbar.

GOAL SQUAD

Leo sank to his knees. Olli threw himself face down on the grass.

"C'mon!" Frankie ran over, pulling Olli up. "Keep going. We need to score."

But as they played on, everything went wrong. The team was falling apart. They were working as solo players rather than a strike force. Leo and Olli were both so focused on the goal that they forgot about working together. Leo tried, but every time he tried to catch Olli's eye, the other striker was always looking at the ball. Tommy was marching up and down the edge of the pitch, calling out orders, but the wind kept whipping his voice away.

Then, with ten minutes to go, Mo was brought crashing to the ground by the Sharks' right back.

The whistle blew.

Foul!

Win the Cup!

Free-kick to the Tigers.

This was their chance!

Leo picked up the ball and placed it down where the free-kick was going to be taken. He always took the free-kicks near the goal.

He backed away from the ball to take a run-up. When he turned round, Olli was blocking him.

"What are you doing?" said Leo. "Get out of the way. I need to take the free-kick."

GOAL SQUAD

"You always take the free-kicks," said Olli through gritted teeth.

"Yes, I'm the best at them," said Leo. "I've scored five this season."

Olli came closer. "It's my turn to take one." Then he shoved Leo in the chest.

Leo's head went really hot, and he shoved Olli back.

Frankie tried to jump in between them, but it was no good – they were shoving each other harder and harder.

"You two! OFF!" Tommy Socket ran on to the pitch, eyes sparking. "I won't have that behaviour from my players." He pointed from Olli to Leo. "I'm subbing you both off. Right now!"

Chapter 8

Leo kept his head down as they left the pitch, cheeks burning.

Olli threw his arms in the air as he approached the sideline.

GOAL SQUAD

"I can't believe I'm being taken off," he cried. "All because this guy wouldn't let me take the free-kick." He jabbed a muddy finger towards Leo.

Leo went quietly over to the bench, put his tracksuit back on, grabbed a woolly hat from his bag and pulled it down to cover up his entire face.

"Now he's hiding," he heard Olli continue. "Look what you've done! You've lost us the game and now we'll get relegated."

"Stop this, Olli," said Tommy. "This is both your fault. Now sit down over there away from Leo. Watch the game and calm down."

Leo heard Olli stomp away, and then the bench creaked. He peeled off the woolly hat to take a better look. Back on the pitch, Frankie was standing over the ball, waiting to take the free-kick.

Win the Cup!

"Can everyone get on with the match," said the ref, checking his watch.

He pointed at Frankie to take the free-kick and blew hard on his whistle.

PEEEEEEEEEEPPPPPPPPPPPPPPPPPPP!

Leo crossed his fingers, his legs and then his feet just to make extra sure that Frankie had all the luck he could send over.

GOAL SQUAD

"C'mon, Frankie," whispered Leo. "You can do it."

Frankie leaned down, flicked a tuft of grass off the ball, then took a few steps back. He stood perfectly still with his arms by his side, and then took in three deep breaths. He closed his eyes.

Leo felt sure his friend was imagining the ball flying into the top left-hand corner of the goal.

Then Frankie started his run-up. He struck the ball ... hard. It made a satisfying pinging noise as it launched into the air.

Yes! The ball cleared the wall of four players that the Sharks had arranged to block the goal.

Then the ball started to bend towards the top left-hand corner. Frankie had put some extra swerve on his shot.

Win the Cup!

The crowd fell silent as the ball cut through the air. Leo found himself getting to his feet as he watched. The next few seconds would be crucial.

The Sharks' goalkeeper was in trouble. He had taken the slightest step to the right just after Frankie had hit the ball. Now he was having to scramble to get across to the left-hand side of the goal. He wasn't going to make it in time – the ball was going too fast.

THWACCCCCKKKKKKKKK! The ball smashed against the top of the crossbar.

SLAAAAAPPPPPPPPPPPP! It bounced back out and hit the diving goalkeeper on his back as he flung himself across the goal.

SCCCCHHHHRRRRRIINNNNNKKKKK! The ball arced back towards the empty goal and nestled in the net.

Win the Cup!

Tigers 1   Sharks 0

The Tigers' crowd went wild. The Sharks' crowd did not.

Frankie gave a casual nod, then crossed his hands and rubbed his arms while puffing out his cheeks.

The rest of the team weren't so casual. They threw themselves at him, tumbling into a massive pile of celebratory limbs.

Leo leaped into the air and gave the sky a big punch.

⚽

The Tigers battled on for the rest of the game, holding off wave after wave of the Sharks' attacks to keep the score at 1–0. It felt like they had been playing for five hours.

Then they heard the sweetest sound as the referee blew the final whistle.

GOAL SQUAD

Most of the team fell to the grass, exhausted. Immediately, Frankie and Mo ran over to Leo.

"What are the scores," they said at the same time.

"You what?" Leo asked, confused.

"The scores of the other games?" Mo gasped. "To see if we've stayed up and qualified for the end-of-season cup."

Leo had totally forgotten about the other matches. He ran over to Tommy Socket, who was holding his phone up to the sky and furiously scrolling up and down the screen.

"Hang on a minute, boys," said Tommy. "I'm trying to get a signal."

Leo, Frankie and Mo

Win the Cup!

hopped from one foot to the other. Leo could feel his armpits prickling with sweat.

The rest of the team huddled round their coach as he spun in circles with his phone in the air.

Everything seemed to go silent as he scrolled again and again. Finally, the screen came alive. "At last!" He peered so close that his nose nearly touched the phone, then he punched the air. "We aren't relegated!"

Everyone cheered and gave each other fist bumps and high fives.

"But what about the cup?" Leo said. They might not be relegated, but had they qualified for the cup? That's what this had all been for ... hadn't it?

Tommy stared at his phone and refreshed it again. Then he held out the screen for the team to see.

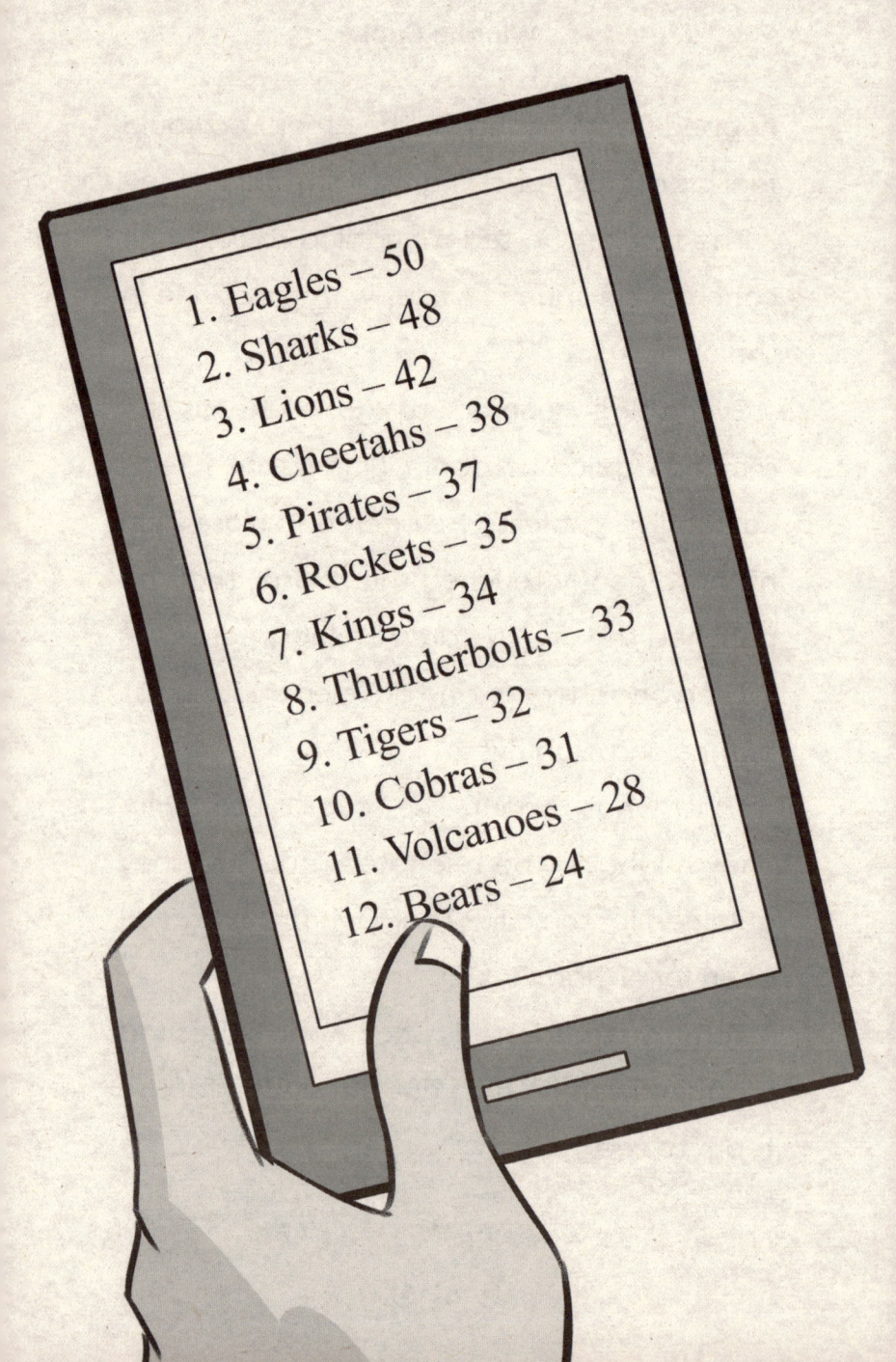

Win the Cup!

The Tigers were sitting in ninth position, just one place outside the qualification for the end-of-season cup.

Everyone fell silent.

Leo should have been happy that the Tigers had survived relegation, but he had really wanted to play in the cup, to win it and give the trophy a big kiss. Like all the top players did when they won a massive trophy.

"Sorry, lads," said Tommy. "It looks like we just missed out this year. But at least we didn't get releg—" He suddenly stopped and looked at his phone as it buzzed in his hand. "Whoa, wait up! My phone signal must have dropped out. I think that league table is wrong – it looks like there was a last-minute penalty at the Thunderbolts."

The team crowded round the phone.

GOAL SQUAD

Leo could just about see the edge of the screen and a few precious words:

Thunderbolts 2   Pirates 1
Penalty to the Pirates...

Leo knew the eighth-placed Thunderbolts were just above the Tigers in the table. If the Pirates drew with the Thunderbolts then the Tigers would jump above them and take eighth position. Then they had a place in the end-of-season cup.

"Refresh it again, Coach," said Frankie.

Tommy pulled his thumb down across the phone's glass. The screen went blank and a rotating circle appeared.

"Hold it up in the air!" cried Mo.

Tommy held the phone above his head, angling the screen down so they could see.

Win the Cup!

The circle disappeared, the screen went white and some words slowly appeared.

Thunderbolts... 2...

Pirates... 2

GOAL SQUAD

"WOOOOOOOOOOOOOOOOOOOOO-HOOOOOOOOOOOO!" shouted Tommy, throwing his phone on the ground to rip off his tracksuit top. He sprinted down the pitch, swinging the jacket above his head.

The team watched him for a few seconds. Then Leo took off his tracksuit top and swung it round his head too. "C'mon, let's all do this," he said, sprinting after their coach. Behind him, he could hear the others whoop and holler. Soon, there was a whole team of players with their tops circling in the air.

"Looks a bit cold to me," said someone's mum as Leo ran past. But it didn't matter.

The Tigers were going to the cup!

Chapter 9

The end-of-season cup was played on Saturday and Sunday at the Walton Green training ground. Leo had been there before and knew that it had lots of pitches all next to each other.

Win the Cup!

If the Tigers won a quarter-final game on Saturday morning, they would play their semi-final on Saturday afternoon.

If they won the semi-final, they would play the final on Sunday afternoon. It was hopefully going to be a very busy weekend for the Tigers' players.

The quarter-final match against the Cheetahs was one of the easiest matches the Tigers had played all season.

The Cheetahs' goalkeeper was sent off in the first half for calling the referee "delulu", and his place was taken by a defender who wasn't a very good goalkeeper.

The Tigers were 3–0 up at half-time, and Mo had scored a hat-trick – left foot, right foot and then one off his knee.

Leo was desperate to get on the scoresheet. He had to get some form back for the semi-final and hopefully the final. It felt like he hadn't scored a proper goal in ages.

Late in the second half, Leo got his chance. Mo was dazzling the Cheetahs' defenders with all kinds of amazing tricks. They couldn't get near him. *No wonder he's been scouted by Westwood Flyers*, thought Leo.

His friend skipped past two diving tackles, got to the byline and crossed a lovely ball straight to Leo on the edge of the area.

Leo could feel a surge of energy course through his body from his head all the way down to his boots. He knew exactly what to do.

He chested Mo's cross down on to his right foot and flicked it on to his much more powerful left foot. He then volleyed it as hard as he could towards the goal.

Win the Cup!

ZINNNNNNNNNNNNNGGGGGGGGGGGG! screamed the ball as it supercharged through the air like a rocket.

SCCHHHRRRRRIIIINNNKKKKKKKKKKK! It rattled into the top corner of the net. The keeper dived totally the wrong way and ended up in a heap on the pitch.

GOAL SQUAD

Tigers 4 Cheetahs 0.

What a goal!

Mo and Frankie sprinted over to Leo and lifted him up on to their shoulders. Leo punched the air. That was one of the best goals he had ever scored!

Even Olli nodded his approval from the other side of the pitch.

⚽

The semi-final against the Pirates was a much tougher game – but really boring. More boring than Leo watching his mum paint a large white wall white.

The score at full time was 0-0. The Tigers and Pirates had both struggled to have shots on goal.

Frankie was all over the pitch, blocking shots and making tackles. He was covered in mud – legs, hands, face and even his hair.

Win the Cup!

He would need a long shower afterwards.

In the cup, a draw at full time meant only one thing – a penalty shoot-out.

Five penalties for each team and, if it was still a draw at the end of the five, it would go to sudden death. Sudden death meant if one team scored and the other missed, then the scoring team would win. Even the thought of it made Leo feel sick.

GOAL SQUAD

"Right then, guys," said Tommy Socket as the team huddled round. "This is your moment. We've practised penalties. Just imagine you're taking them in practice and you will score. No tricks, just blast the ball low and hard. Who wants to go first?"

Frankie's hand shot up. Tommy scribbled down his name. Mo said he'd take the second one, Josh wanted the third and Noah the fourth.

Nobody put their hand up for the fifth penalty.

"I need another penalty taker," said Tommy. "Or I'll have to pick one of you at random."

Leo glanced at Olli. He was staring hard at the ground, standing right at the back. For once, he didn't have anything to say.

Win the Cup!

Leo knew he was the team's best striker, and usually took penalties, but he was feeling extra nervous. He gritted his teeth. *Just be brave*, he told himself. Someone had to take the crucial fifth penalty! He raised his hand.

"Excellent," said Tommy. "Thank you, Leo." He scribbled down the final name.

"If we go past five penalties and into sudden death, then I will need more volunteers, but I know Frankie, Mo, Josh, Noah and Leo can all score. And then Josh might be able to save one or two."

Leo felt a wave of butterflies start flying around in his stomach. He'd taken penalties before, but this was a much bigger deal. If they won this penalty shoot-out, they'd be in the cup final.

The Tigers gathered in the centre circle

and linked arms with each other in a circle. Then they faced the goal. This was it.

Frankie went up first... GOAL. Blasted straight in the bottom left-hand corner just like Tommy had said.

Tigers 1 Pirates 0.

The Pirates' big number nine was up next... GOAL. Josh went the wrong way.

Tigers 1 Pirates 1.

Then Mo... GOAL. Top left-hand corner.

Tigers 2 Pirates 1.

Pirates number three... GOAL. Josh got a fingertip to it, but it wasn't enough.

Tigers 2 Pirates 2.

Win the Cup!

Now it was Josh. A goalkeeper taking a penalty was rare, as they were usually only good with their hands, not their feet.

Luckily for the Tigers, Josh was also good with his feet.

BANG! Top of the net, the best penalty so far...

Tigers 3 Pirates 2.

The Pirates' number seven... GOAL. Too fast for Josh...

Tigers 3 Pirates 3.

Next for the Tigers was Noah... GOAL! The ball hit the post but still went in. Lucky.

Tigers 4 Pirates 3.

Up stepped the Pirates' number ten. He bit his lip as he placed the ball on the spot, then moved it to the side, then moved it back again, then moved it to the side again.

GOAL SQUAD

The ref blew his whistle and the number ten started his run-up, and then smashed the ball ... high over the crossbar and into a field of cows behind the goal.

It was still Tigers 4 Pirates 3.

If Leo scored, the Tigers would be in the final.

He took a deep breath and rubbed his palms together. They had never been this sweaty before. Then he started his walk from the halfway line to the penalty spot.

It must have only taken five seconds, but it felt like two hours. The longest walk ever.

Win the Cup!

In his head, he could hear Tommy saying, "Blast it low and hard!" Then his grandad saying the same thing, then his mum saying the same thing, then his Uncle Derek saying, "Does anyone want a burger?"

He scrunched up his eyes and shook his head. He had to get rid of Uncle Derek.

He finally got to the penalty spot and placed the ball down, making sure he didn't fiddle with it like the Pirates' number ten who had missed. He took five steps back and waited for the ref to blow the whistle. Everything fell quiet. Leo was sure he could hear his heart beating louder and louder. The goal suddenly looked tiny and the goalkeeper massive.

PEEEEEEEEEEEEEPPPPPPPPPPPP! went the whistle.

Leo took a deep breath, along with one last look at the goal, and charged towards the ball.

WWWWWWWWWWHHHAACCCCCCKKKK! Leo smashed the ball as hard as he could.

It flew into the corner of the net and Leo sank to his knees with relief.

"GOOOOOOOOOOOAAAAAAAAAAAALLLLLLLLLLLLLLLLL!"

Tommy and their supporters flooded the pitch. Even Leo's mum ran on! Everyone whooped as they jumped on Leo.

"Great penalty," said Frankie later as they

headed to the changing rooms. "I knew you'd get us into the final."

"We wouldn't have got to penalties without you, Frankie," Leo said. "You were the man of the match."

Frankie's cheeks turned pink.

"Now we have to win the final tomorrow," Leo said, his mind already racing ahead. "I wonder who we are playing?"

"It's either the Sharks again or the Eagles. They were playing each other in the other semi-final," replied Frankie. "But their game finished before ours and I didn't see who won. I hope it's not the Eagles. They're tough."

"So are the Sharks," added Leo.

They shook their heads at each other.

"It's going to be a really hard final," Frankie said, ducking into the changing room. Leo

Win the Cup!

stood back and watched his friends sitting on the benches, laughing. It wasn't over yet... He hoped everyone would still be laughing tomorrow. And maybe Tommy Socket would get them all fish and chips if they won.

Chapter 10

Leo hardly slept that night. The butterflies were back in his stomach. In the morning, he couldn't eat his breakfast, even though his mum had made pancakes.

Win the Cup!

He got to the pitch and began warming up with the rest of the team. Everyone was quiet. Even Frankie and Mo looked nervous.

Leo gazed over to the other side of the pitch, to the team they were playing in the final. They wore the green-and-black kit of the Eagles. They had beaten the Sharks 4–3.

The Eagles' big number five was jogging up and down, warming up. He looked even bigger and stronger than the last time Leo had played against him. He had cut his hair into a mohawk too and coloured it bright green.

GOAL SQUAD

"This is my last game for the Tigers," Mo said, coming up to join Leo. "We have to win. As long as I set you up right, you can score."

Leo had almost forgotten that Mo would be joining Westwood Flyers after the final. He was sad it was their last match together.

"You know we'll play together again," said Mo, as though reading his thoughts. "Westwood Flyers will see how good you are. Before you know it, you'll be with me at the academy. Frankie too."

Leo fist-bumped Mo. Wouldn't it be great if they could all play together at the Westwood Flyers academy? But first, they had a cup final to go and win.

⚽

Leo and Frankie had been right. It was a really tough game. The Eagles were 1–0 up at half-time, and the Tigers were struggling

Win the Cup!

to get hold of the ball.

The Eagles' number five was so good he was managing to stop both Leo and Olli from having any shots.

Leo and Olli had to work together in the second half or they would lose the match.

While they were having a half-time drink, Leo went and sat next to Olli.

"I know we're not the best of friends," he began. "But we are on the same team."

"So?" replied Olli.

"So, we have to start playing as a strike partnership, not just single strikers. Neither of us can beat that number five on our own."

"I think I can," said Olli.

Leo took a deep breath. "You can't," he said. "And I can't either. He's too good."

Olli went quiet and stared at the pitch.

"So, what do we do?" he said after a while.

GOAL SQUAD

"We start passing to each other. It's the only way we can get past him," said Leo. "We both want to win the cup. It doesn't matter who scores the goals. We just have to win the game."

Olli pulled at a few blades of grass. "OK," he said. "It's a deal."

Leo stuck out his fist, and Olli bumped his against it. Finally, they were working together!

Win the Cup!

The second half was much better for the Tigers.

The big number five had to mark both Leo and Olli at the same time. The other Eagles' defenders weren't helping out and Number Five's face had grown bright red.

The Tigers' equalizer was a bit of a surprise. Their defender, Noah, scored it.

He seemed to be crossing the ball into the Eagles' area, but their goalkeeper got into the wrong position and the ball looped over his head and into the net.

Tigers 1 Eagles 1.

Noah had never scored for the Tigers before! He was so shocked that he fell over backwards.

The game continued and still neither team could score the winning goal. Leo could see

GOAL SQUAD

Tommy looking at his watch. There couldn't be much time left.

Both sides were looking really tired. After all, this was their third game in two days. Leo's leg muscles were starting to hurt. Nobody wanted to go to extra time or penalties.

The number five was still locked in, though. Leo had to find a way past him.

Frankie won the ball on the halfway line and passed it to Noah who was now flying up the right side of the pitch. That lucky goal had given him loads of extra energy.

Noah played a lovely cross-field pass all the way over to Mo on the left of the pitch.

Mo volleyed into the area, but it was headed back out by the number five ... straight to Leo.

Leo dribbled round the edge of the area.

"I'm coming for you," said the big number

Win the Cup!

five as he ran towards Leo.

But Leo was ready for him. He juggled the ball from his right foot to his left, and then chipped it into the air just as the number five slid in for a crunching tackle.

Leo hopped over the tackle and was clear! All he had to do now was lob the keeper, lifting the ball over his head to score the winning goal. Easy ... or was it? What happened if the keeper punched it away or if Leo hit the bar?

Then he saw Olli running into the area behind the keeper.

Leo had two choices. He could take the glory with a lovely lob. Or he could pass it to Olli for a simple tap-in. He remembered what he had said to Olli at half-time.

It doesn't matter who scores the goals. We just have to win the game.

Decision made. Option two was the safer one.

He rolled the ball into Olli's path and watched as his teammate smashed it into the empty net.

Tigers 2 Eagles 1.

Everyone charged over to Olli and celebrated with him. Leo was about to run over too, when he was suddenly sent flying to the ground.

The big number five was so angry about

Win the Cup!

being tricked that he'd pushed Leo in the back.

PEEEEEEEEEPPPPPPP! PEEEEEEEEPPPPP! PEEEEEEEEPPPPPP! went the ref's whistle.

"You!" shouted the ref, pulling out a red card. "Number Five! Red card. Off. Right now."

"But I never!" said the number five, putting his hands together.

The ref pointed to the changing rooms.

The number five trudged off the pitch.

Leo rolled over on to his back and saw a figure standing over him, holding out a hand.

It was Olli.

"Nice pass," Olli said, pulling Leo up on to his feet.

"No problem," Leo replied, grinning. "I knew you'd score."

"I wouldn't have scored if you hadn't tricked that defender. Sorry about all the stuff earlier in the season. You were right – we can work really well together as a great strike force next season."

Yet again, Olli had a lot to say – but this time, it all made sense!

Before Leo could say anything back the final whistle blew.

A huge cheer erupted.

Leo and Olli looked at each other and laughed. "WE JUST WON THE CUP! WOOOOOO-HOOOO!"

Leo's mum ran on to the pitch and gave Leo a massive kiss on the cheek. "I knew

Win the Cup!

you could do it!" she gasped. He wished she'd told him that a week ago!

"Muuuuuuuummmm," said Leo, trying to pull away.

The Westwood Flyers academy scout appeared at the side of the pitch holding a big silver trophy. It was much bigger than the one Leo had seen in his dreams.

Leo pushed their captain forward. "Go on. Go and collect the cup."

"You come too," said Frankie, pulling Leo with him. "We couldn't have done it without you and that amazing assist."

Leo looked towards Tommy Socket, who gave them two thumbs up to both lift the cup. He really was one of the best coaches in the whole world ever!

The scout handed Frankie and Leo the cup. "Keep playing like that and I'll be back to

GOAL SQUAD

scout you for Westwood Flyers next season," he said. Leo hoped he would keep his promise.

He looked around the pitch at all the watching faces. Everyone was smiling and clapping. The Tigers had done it – together, they'd won the cup.

Win the Cup!

Leo and Frankie grinned and grabbed a handle of the cup each. Then they turned to face the crowd in front of them.

"WOOOOOOOOOOOOOOOOOOOOO-HOOOOOOOOOOOOOOOOOOO," said everyone in a rising, excited noise.

Leo and Frankie crouched down.

"On the count of three," Frankie whispered to Leo. "One ... two ... three!"

GOAL SQUAD

The two of them leaped into the air, thrusting the cup above them as the crowd burst into cheers and applause.

Leo thought his head would pop off with excitement.

"I could get used to this!" he cried, balancing the cup on his head. It was the first cup the Tigers had ever won. But as he looked around, Leo couldn't help wondering ... what would they win next?

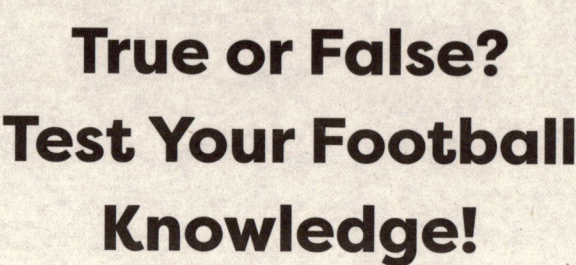

True or False? Test Your Football Knowledge!

1. **The World Cup trophy is made of solid gold.**
    - ⚽ TRUE! It weighs as much as a small cat – about six kilograms!

2. **Football players can run up to thirteen kilometres during one match.**
    - ⚽ TRUE! That's like running from one end of a city to the other!

3. **Only five countries have ever won the World Cup.**
    - ⚽ FALSE! Eight different countries have won it, but Brazil has won the most times – five victories!

4. **The fastest World Cup goal was scored in just eleven seconds.**
    - ⚽ TRUE! Imagine – the match had barely started!

5. **Goalkeepers wear different coloured jerseys just because they like to stand out.**
   - ⚽ FALSE! They wear different colours so the referee can easily tell them apart from other players.

6. **Old football balls used to get heavier when it rained.**
   - ⚽ TRUE! The first World Cup balls were made of leather and soaked up water like a sponge!

7. **The youngest World Cup player ever was only thirteen years old.**
   - ⚽ FALSE! The youngest was seventeen – still super young though!

8. **Over half the people on Earth watched the 2018 World Cup.**
   - ⚽ TRUE! Football really is the world's most popular sport!

9. **Every World Cup uses the exact same ball.**
   - ⚽ FALSE! Each World Cup has its own special ball with a unique design and name!

10. **Almost 200,000 people once watched a World Cup match in one stadium.**
    - ⚽ TRUE! This happened in Brazil in 1950 – imagine that huge crowd!

Who Wrote *Goal Squad: Win the Cup?*

After discovering he was too tall and heavy to be a jockey, **Scott Allen** turned his attention to football. His favourite team is West Ham. He started following them when he was five and it's been a roller coaster ever since. His favourite football players are – in no order – Declan Rice, Luděk Mikloško, Phil Parkes, Julian Dicks, Ray Stewart, Bobby Moore, Alvin Martin, Billy Bonds, Sir Trevor Brooking, Alan Devonshire and Paolo Di Canio. His published books include middle-grade novel *Llama United* and its sequel, *Llamas Go Large*, and children's non-fiction book *On Your Marks, Get Set, Gold!*